Practical Pre-School Books

Outstanding Early Years Provision in practice Book 2

WITHDRAWN

by Nicola Scade

Contents

For Jasmine – A curious little explorer at the start of her adventures.

Published by Practical Pre-School Books, A Division of MA Education Ltd, St. Jude's Church, Dulwich Road, Herne Hill, London, SE24 0PB.

Tel: 020 7738 5454 www.practicalpreschoolbooks.com

© MA Education Ltd 2017

Design: Alison Cutler **fonthill**creative 01722 717043

Disclaimer: Practitioners should take the recommended health and safety precautions with equipment provided and check beforehand for any allergies to materials. It is the responsibility of the practitioners to ensure that the resources provided are suitable for all children in the setting and necessary risk assessments should be carried out where appropriate.

ISBN 978-1-909280-97-7

Introduction

Who this book is for

Outstanding Early Years Provision in Practice - Book 2 follows on from the first book by sharing further exciting and stimulating activities created using simple ideas, everyday resources and by adapting activities that have worked well in the past. The book aims to support all early years practitioners, particularly those working with children aged 3-5. It is also ideal resource material for students taking the PGCE course or any early years education qualification.

Observing children as they engage with the resources that you have provided for them, with looks of wonder and excitement on their faces, has to be one of the most rewarding parts of being an early years practitioner. It is fascinating to see how their investigations develop and how they utilise and adapt the provision, following their own paths of curiosity. Often, they will move far beyond our original intentions for an activity, helping to further shape and develop it over time.

Sharing good practice by visiting other settings is a particularly useful way of inspiring and generating ideas. The photos throughout the book and the feedback from children come from a range of real early years settings, showcasing creativity and resourcefulness and truly inspiring comments from the little leaners!

How to use this book

Book 2 follows the same clear and accessible format of the first title in the set. It offers concise text with the emphasis on bright and detailed photographs, supporting you to enhance your learning environment, either by recreating what you see in the pictures or by adapting it to suit your children.

For each activity you will find a **list of resources**, a **challenge section** with ideas on how to extend the provision, **observations of children** including their direct quotes and **links to the current Early Years Framework**.

You will find an outline of how each activity can be used to support children's development across the **seven areas of learning** and how the activity can enable children to demonstrate and develop the characteristics of effective learning – as defined in the EYFS Framework.

The **areas of learning tables** at the back of the book may help you plan more effectively.

Enhance your provision

These simple steps will help guide you as you use this book to develop your provision:

- Be guided by the children
- Utilise what you already have but in new ways
- Use real and authentic resources wherever possible
- Continually check and monitor the effectiveness of the provision
- Ensure that there are opportunities for extension and challenge.

"In planning and guiding children's activities, practitioners must reflect on the different ways that children learn and reflect these in their practice. The three characteristics of effective teaching and learning are:

- **Playing and exploring** – children investigate and experience things, and 'have a go';

- **Active learning** – children concentrate and keep on trying if they encounter difficulties, and enjoy achievements; and

- **Creating and thinking critically** – children have and develop their own ideas, make links between ideas, and develop strategies for doing things."

Statutory Framework for The Early Years Foundation Stage 2017, Section 1.9, P10.

And finally… Take snaps of the projects and share your good practice!

Home grown resources

Chapter One: Exploration and investigation

Key Areas of EYFS developed in this chapter:

- Physical Development

- Mathematics

- Understanding the World

- Expressive Arts and Design.

Activities for this chapter are:

- Heave ho
- Frozen florist
- Easy peasy lemon squeezy
- Sensory bottles
- Entangled
- Transient art.

Useful resources for activities in this chapter:

- Assorted size rocks, sticks, stones and logs and other interesting natural objects
- Flowers and plants
- Clipboards
- Picture frames
- Cooking utensils
- Containers and plastic bottles
- Water
- Paint

- Glitter
- Coloured tape.

The characteristics of effective learning: Playing and exploring, Active learning and Creating and thinking critically, describe **how** children learn rather than **what** they learn. Gathering this information through observation and interaction allows practitioners to effectively plan and create an environment that is accessible, challenging and of interest to all children. It goes without saying that children are more likely to attempt an activity if it is interesting to them. Opportunities for hands on multi-sensory exploration and investigation should be available across the provision, enabling children to develop and demonstrate these characteristics of effective learning.

By providing resources and open-ended activities that spark children's curiosity we can encourage them to engage and take risks. Activities where children can observe things closely, test out their own ideas, problem solve and think critically should be plentiful. It is through such opportunities that children learn to make sense of the world around them.

Exploration and investigation activities also help children to:
- Think independently and make decisions for themselves.
- Focus their attention on a particular interest or line of enquiry.
- Set their own rules and challenges.
- Work collaboratively and build friendships.

Resources for such activities do not need to be expensive or elaborate. Simple resources presented in the right way are often the most effective. Cardboard boxes, buckets, crates and fabric with no fixed purpose, provide endless opportunities for creative and imaginative play.

The real-life quotes from children in this chapter (and throughout the book) give an insight into how each activity can contribute to children's learning across the seven areas of learning.

You will find specific links and resources for each activity in this chapter.

'Cool' Investigations!

Got It!

Heave ho

Setting up the provision

Method
Secure a bucket or basket to one end of a rope, loop it over a pillar, post or climbing frame and secure the other end at the bottom, creating a basic pulley system.

Resources
- Bucket or Basket
- Rope
- A stable pillar, post or climbing frame
- Objects/materials for transporting.

Handy hints
- Recycle old containers. Often resources such as powder paints and craft materials come in light weight

"I think I'm going to need help with this load. It is so heavy."

plastic buckets that could be used as the vessel.
- Use the pulley to transport horizontally as well as vertically, pulling your vessel along a fence for example or across a sand or water tray.
- Throw your rope over a tree branch and secure around the base of the tree for added adventure.

Questions to help you extend the activity and to ensure challenge

Questions for you:
- Are the children able to choose the resources they want to transport and compare the weight of?

- How can children record the results of their investigations?

How does the activity enable children to develop and demonstrate the characteristics of effective learning?

Characteristic of effective learning	The enabling environment: Heave ho
Playing and exploring – engagement ● Finding out and exploring. ● Playing with what they know. ● Being willing to 'have a go'.	Children can investigate the resources and discover for themselves how the activity works. The activity is open ended.
Active learning – motivation ● Being involved and concentrating. ● Keeping trying. ● Enjoying achieving what they set out to do.	The activity presents an immediate challenge. Children have the opportunity to problem solve. If the pulley gets stuck or tangled or if the weight of the object is too heavy for example.
Creating and thinking critically – thinking ● Having their own ideas. ● Making links. ● Choosing ways to do things.	The activity relies on team work, listening to each other and building trust. Children can decide what they want to transport and have the opportunity to explore the best way to do it, making predictions and testing their ideas. Children can compare and discuss how difficult it is to lift the weight of the objects in the bucket both with and without the pulley.

Strength and determination

How the activity can support children's development across the 7 areas of learning

Areas of Learning: Personal, Social and Emotional Development

Children have the opportunity to:
- Take into consideration the ideas of others.
- Work as a team.
- Resolve any conflicts that may arise as they negotiate how to use and share the equipment.

Areas of Learning: Communication and Language

Children have the opportunity to:
- Develop their vocabulary being introduced to key words such as *pull, transport, lift, heavy, light, empty, full, raise, lower*.
- Describe and explain how the pulley system works.
- Ask questions about how something works.
- Respond to simple instructions.

Areas of Learning: Physical Development

Children have the opportunity to:
- Build up their strength.
- Control the amount of force that they exert.
- Develop their coordination.
- Demonstrate an awareness of the importance of safety when using the equipment.

Areas of Learning: Literacy

Children have the opportunity to:
- Draw and label their equipment.
- Write lists of heavy and light objects.

Areas of Learning: Mathematics

Children have the opportunity to:
- Compare and sort objects by shape, size and weight.
- Record using tables and charts.
- Use positional language.

Areas of Learning: Understanding the World

Children have the opportunity to:
- Make careful observations about how the pulley system works and ask appropriate questions.

Areas of Learning: Expressive Arts and Design

Children have the opportunity to:
- Engage in imaginative play.

- Could the activity be used within role play to transport relevant props?

Questions for the children:
- What happens when you pull down on the rope?

- Can you find something that you think would be very light to transport?

- Which object is the heaviest and how do you know?

 "I'm so strong, let's put twenty blocks in the bucket. I can pull it all the way up."

 "Let's all pull together and the rope will go up quicker."

Successful team work

A 'pretty' good investigation

Frozen florist

Targeted areas of learning:
Understanding the World and
Expressive Arts and Design

Setting up the provision

Method
Mix a selection of brightly coloured flowers with water
and place in assorted sized containers in the freezer.
Once frozen remove the containers from the freezer
and set up an area for open ended observation and
investigation.

Resources
- Assorted sized containers
- A variety of colourful flowers
- A freezer
- Resources that the children might suggest for helping
  to release the flowers from the ice such as towels or
  pens and pencils to use as chisels.

Handy hints
- Support the children to explore what happens when
  they pour salt onto the ice. How does this compare
  with sugar or sand for example?

- Add herbs such as basil and mint to the water for an
  added sensory experience.

- Use the leftover flowery water for perfume or potion
  making.

Questions to help you extend the activity and to ensure challenge

Questions for you:
- Could you challenge the children to follow recipe cards
  with instructions for particular flower quantities and
  colours?

- What tools will you have available for the children to
  investigate the ice melting? What will the children
  suggest?

How the activity can support children's development across the 7 areas of learning

Areas of Learning: Personal, Social and Emotional Development

Children have the opportunity to:

- Share resources.
- Select and use resources with help.
- Express their own ideas and preferences.

Areas of Learning: Communication and Language

Children have the opportunity to:

- Develop their vocabulary being introduced to key words such as *freeze, melt, solid, liquid, hot, cold, temperature, change.*
- Describe how the ice feels and how it looks as it changes state.
- Follow simple instructions.

Areas of Learning: Physical Development

Children have the opportunity to:

- Strengthen their fine motor skills using tweezers to carefully retrieve the flowers from the ice.
- Use small tools to chisel and chip away at the ice.

Areas of Learning: Literacy

Children have the opportunity to:

- Draw and label their ice creations.
- Make links with familiar stories, songs and rhymes.

Areas of Learning: Mathematics

Children have the opportunity to:

- Follow recipe cards with instructions for particular flower quantities and colours.
- Investigate capacity and volume.

Areas of Learning: Understanding the World

Children have the opportunity to:

- Make careful observations, investigating changes of state and beginning to understand about solids and liquids.

Areas of Learning: Expressive Arts and Design

Children have the opportunity to:

- Explore and compare colour, smell and texture.
- Manipulate resources and tools purposefully.
- Express their own preferences.

What treasures will you find to freeze next?

Questions for the children:

- How can we get the flowers out of the ice?

- Can you describe how the ice is changing?

- What else would you like to freeze?

"I have 2 pink flowers and 1 red flower in my pot."

"My hands are hot and making it melt."

How does the activity enable children to develop and demonstrate the characteristics of effective learning?

Characteristic of effective learning	The enabling environment: Frozen florist
Playing and exploring – engagement ● Finding out and exploring. ● Playing with what they know. ● Being willing to 'have a go'.	The activity is multi-sensory and intriguing. Children have the opportunity to play and explore with familiar objects and materials but in new ways.
Active learning – motivation ● Being involved and concentrating. ● Keeping trying. ● Enjoying achieving what they set out to do.	Children have the opportunity to observe the changes to the ice over time, maintaining their concentration for a sustained period. Children may need to persevere with the methods they choose to excavate the flowers from the ice.
Creating and thinking critically – thinking ● Having their own ideas. ● Making links. ● Choosing ways to do things.	Children can make predictions and test their own ideas, suggesting and finding further resources they might need for their investigation. Children can suggest follow up activities based on their own interests.

Beautifully preserved but how can we free them?

Squish, Squash, Squeeze, I'll have a lemonade please!

Easy peasy lemon squeezy

 "Oranges are very good for you, they make your skin and bones healthy and shiny."

Setting up the provision

Method

Set up a tray with halved lemons and oranges and a variety of tools that can be used to extract their juice. Add some cups, mixing pots and spoons.

Resources

- Oranges and lemons
- A selection of juicing tools – squeezers and reamers
- Cups and pots
- Funnels
- Sieves
- Cocktail umbrellas/straws.

Handy hints

- Following appropriate health and safety measures you could use the juice for tasting.

- Or add washing up liquid and froth up some bubbles for your own drinks factory (without the tasting!)

- Support children to compare the effectiveness of each tool for juicing, including their own hands.

How does the activity enable children to develop and demonstrate the characteristics of effective learning?

Characteristic of effective learning	The enabling environment: Easy peasy lemon squeezy
Playing and exploring – engagement ● Finding out and exploring. ● Playing with what they know. ● Being willing to 'have a go'.	The activity is multi-sensory and allows children to investigate what is familiar to them whilst learning how to use new tools and techniques.
Active learning – motivation ● Being involved and concentrating. ● Keeping trying. ● Enjoying achieving what they set out to do.	Children have the opportunity to persevere when learning how to use new tools and techniques. Children will be motivated to create their own drinks/ mixtures and can engage in imaginative play.
Creating and thinking critically – thinking ● Having their own ideas. ● Making links. ● Choosing ways to do things.	Children can decide what type of drink they want to make and develop a narrative to go alongside their play. Children can predict and test out which tool is the most effective for juicing and experiment with their own methods.

Awaken the senses

How the activity can support children's development across the 7 areas of learning

Areas of Learning: Personal, Social and Emotional Development

Children have the opportunity to:
- Share resources.
- Develop the confidence to try new activities and use new tools.

Areas of Learning: Communication and Language

Children have the opportunity to:
- Develop their vocabulary being introduced to key words such as *full, empty, half, whole, twist, turn.*

Areas of Learning: Physical Development

Children have the opportunity to:
- Strengthen their fine motor skills using the different juicing tools and their own hands.
- Handle tools safely.
- Discuss different types of food and begin to categorise.
- Discuss the effects of healthy/unhealthy foods on the body.

Areas of Learning: Literacy

Children have the opportunity to:
- Write ingredient lists.
- Write instructions.
- Write menus.

Areas of Learning: Mathematics

Children have the opportunity to:
- Investigate capacity and volume.
- Explore concepts such as more and less, full and empty, half and whole.

Areas of Learning: Understanding the World

Children have the opportunity to:
- Demonstrate an awareness of cause and effect, understanding how each of the tools works.
- Make careful observations.

Areas of Learning: Expressive Arts and Design

Children have the opportunity to:
- Compare and describe the texture, colour and smell.

Questions to help you extend the activity and to ensure challenge

Questions for you:
- Are there opportunities for writing menus, instructions and ingredient lists?
- Are there opportunities for investigating capacity and volume by providing measuring cylinders for example and assorted sized containers?
- Could you develop a role play area around the activity? A drinks factory or a juice shop for example.

Questions for the children:
- Which cup would you use if you wanted the most lemonade?
- Can you explain which tool was the best juicer?
- Can you write a list of the ingredients needed for your special drink?

 "I'm making lemonade for my birthday party."

 "I have got lots more juice in this cup than in that one."

Moon dust, monster juice or a magic potion?

Sensory bottles

 "Everything in the room looks pink through this bottle."

Setting up the provision

Method

Combine water, glitter, oil and paint, experimenting with the ratios to achieve different effects. Seal the bottles with tape, shake and observe.

Resources

- Empty plastic bottles
- Duct tape
- Pipettes
- Funnels
- Plastic jugs or test tubes for mixing
- Glitter or sequins
- Liquids: water, oil, paint, food colouring.

Handy hints

- Involve children in the process of making the bottles, experimenting with the ratios and combinations of different liquids.

- The bottles can be used as props in role play areas. In a science lab, a drinks factory or a space station for example.

- Add objects to the bottles to make miniature small world scenes.

- Fill your bottles with objects and colours to represent the different seasons. Create a winter bottle with white paint, oil and silver glitter for example.

How the activity can support children's development across the 7 areas of learning

Areas of Learning: Personal, Social and Emotional Development

Children have the opportunity to:

- Share resources.
- Initiate and take turns in conversation.
- Work in a group.

Areas of Learning: Communication and Language

Children have the opportunity to:

- Develop their vocabulary being introduced to key words such *transparent, opaque, heavy, light, empty, full, solid, liquid*.
- Describe what they can see when they look inside and through the bottles.

Areas of Learning: Physical Development

Children have the opportunity to:

- Show an awareness of safety when combining different materials.
- Handle resources with control and precision.

Areas of Learning: Literacy

Children have the opportunity to:

- Write ingredients lists.
- Write instructions.
- Make labels.
- Use the bottles as props for storytelling.

Areas of Learning: Mathematics

Children have the opportunity to:

- Compare the size, shape, weight and colour of the bottles.
- Explore capacity.

Areas of Learning: Understanding the World

Children have the opportunity to:

- Make observations about how different materials react with each other.

Areas of Learning: Expressive Arts and Design

Children have the opportunity to:

- Explore colour mixing.
- Capture experiences with music and dance.

Combining liquids to create his own sensory bottle

Questions to help you extend the activity and to ensure challenge

Questions for you:

- Could the movement in the bottles be used to inspire a dance or music activity?

- Could you use the bottles as story props, encouraging the children to develop a narrative around their fascinating mixture?

Questions for the children:

- Can you describe what you can see?

- Can you describe how the liquid moves as you turn the bottle upside down?

- What/who do you think the liquid might be for?

 "The water is thick inside so you can't see through it."

How does the activity enable children to develop and demonstrate the characteristics of effective learning?

Characteristic of effective learning	The enabling environment: Sensory bottles
Playing and exploring – engagement ● Finding out and exploring. ● Playing with what they know. ● Being willing to 'have a go'.	The activity is vibrant and colourful, encouraging children to come and investigate. Children can explore mixing the liquids, combining them in different ways and observing the effects.
Active learning – motivation ● Being involved and concentrating. ● Keeping trying. ● Enjoying achieving what they set out to do.	Children have the opportunity to spend time observing and discussing what they can see, encouraging sustained concentration. Children will need to concentrate on using the tools carefully as they create their own mixtures.
Creating and thinking critically – thinking ● Having their own ideas. ● Making links. ● Choosing ways to do things.	The bottles can be used as props for storytelling, children can use their imaginations to think of what the liquid might do and who it might be for. The activity allows children to decide how they want to combine different liquids, adapting quantities and observing the effects as they go.

Role play props for young scientists

Over, under, around and through

Entangled

 "We are spiders and have made a giant web."

Setting up the provision

Method

Secure poles or sticks in the ground and tie lengths of coloured tape between them. Ensure that the tapes cross over each other, high and low, creating a maze/trap effect. Start the activity off by modelling this technique for the children. Then support them to extend and develop what you have begun. How will children find their way through? What or who will they trap?

Resources

- Coloured tape
- Sticks, bamboo canes or plant stakes
- Timers.

Handy hints

- Add yellow and black hazard tape to create a danger zone!

- Add sand timers and stop watches for timed challenges. How quickly can children escape? They can compete against each other and themselves.

- As well as a challenging assault course, the activity can inspire imaginative play.

- Place a teddy in the centre for children to rescue.

- Provide spider costumes so that children can get into character as they spin their 'web.'

How does the activity enable children to develop and demonstrate the characteristics of effective learning?

Characteristic of effective learning	The enabling environment: Entangled
Playing and exploring – engagement ● Finding out and exploring. ● Playing with what they know. ● Being willing to 'have a go'.	Children have the opportunity to explore and play outside on a large scale. The activity poses an immediate challenge and is open ended. The activity encourages risk taking.
Active learning – motivation ● Being involved and concentrating. ● Keeping trying. ● Enjoying achieving what they set out to do.	Children will need to persevere when using the materials to build the trap and will be motivated to find the best route to take to escape from it.
Creating and thinking critically – thinking ● Having their own ideas. ● Making links. ● Choosing ways to do things.	The activity can be extended over time. Children can set their own timed challenges. The activity can inspire imaginative play, children can incorporate themes and characters from familiar stories in their play.

The trap is set. Who will you catch?

How the activity can support children's development across the 7 areas of learning

Areas of Learning: Personal, Social and Emotional Development

Children have the opportunity to:
- Play in a group, collaborating and extending ideas.
- Develop the confidence to try new activities.
- Take risks.

Areas of Learning: Communication and Language

Children have the opportunity to:
- Develop their vocabulary being introduced to key words such as *under, over, through, up, down, inside, outside.*
- Give and follow simple instructions.
- Introduce a storyline into their play.

Areas of Learning: Physical Development

Children have the opportunity to:
- Negotiate space successfully, avoiding obstacles.
- Experiment with different ways of moving their whole body.
- Develop their fine motor skills as they use the tape to assemble the trap.

Areas of Learning: Literacy

Children have the opportunity to:
- Draw on themes and characters from familiar stories in their play.

Areas of Learning: Mathematics

Children have the opportunity to:
- Measure time.
- Use positional and directional language.
- Explore colour, pattern and shape.

Areas of Learning: Understanding of the World

Children have the opportunity to:
- Make maps and plans.

Areas of Learning: Expressive Arts and Design

Children have the opportunity to:
- Engage in imaginative play.
- Construct with a purpose in mind.
- Select tools and techniques needed to assemble and join materials together.

Questions to help you extend the activity and to ensure challenge

Questions for you:
- Is key vocabulary displayed, showing positional and directional language?
- Are relevant story books available to inspire and develop children's imaginative play?

Questions for the children:
- Which story book characters could you catch using this trap?
- Who are you escaping from?
- Can you describe the route you took to escape?

"The red lines are electric. If you touch them the alarm will go off and you will be caught."

Escaping from the Big Bad Wolf!

It's all about the process

Transient art

Targeted areas of learning:
Understanding the World
and Expressive Arts and Design

 "I am going to use a shell for a house and some leaves for the clouds."

Setting up the provision

Method

Provide children with the opportunity to select from a range of interesting natural materials. Encourage them to arrange the loose parts into pictures and patterns, either on paper on within a frame. The materials are not fixed down and so there is no permanent end product. This allows children the freedom to rework and refine their masterpieces.

Resources

- Shells, pebbles, rocks, fir cones, fossils, sticks, plants, petals, grass – as many interesting natural materials as you can provide
- Picture frames (paper, plastic or wood- without the glass)
- Paper or card
- Digital camera
- Non-fiction nature books.

Handy hints

- Support children to use a digital camera to photograph the different stages of their work so that they can track and review their creative process – observing how they have adapted and refined their work over time.

- Create a permanent area for self-selection, topping up and changing the materials regularly.

- Cork place mats make a useful face template when arranging materials to make portraits.

How the activity can support children's development across the 7 areas of learning

Areas of Learning: Personal, Social and Emotional Development

Children have the opportunity to:

- Have their own ideas and select materials and resources independently.
- Work on their own individual projects or collaboratively with others.

Areas of Learning: Communication and Language

Children have the opportunity to:

- Maintain attention.
- Talk through what they are doing, organising and clarifying their ideas.

Areas of Learning: Physical Development

Children have the opportunity to:

- Handle and arrange small objects with control and purpose.

Areas of Learning: Literacy

Children have the opportunity to:

- Use information books to find out about the natural materials.
- Create story settings.

Areas of Learning: Mathematics

Children have the opportunity to:

- Explore and compare shape, weight and size.
- Make repeating patterns.

Areas of Learning: Understanding the World

Children have the opportunity to:

- Observe objects carefully, commenting on their features.
- Describe patterns and change.
- Use a digital camera with support.

Areas of Learning: Expressive Arts and Design

Children have the opportunity to:

- Manipulate materials to achieve a planned effect.
- Select appropriate materials and adapt work where necessary.
- Experiment with colour, pattern and design.

A work in progress

Questions to help you extend the activity and to ensure challenge

Questions for you:

- Are there opportunities for children to go outside and gather the natural materials themselves?

- Are there opportunities for children to explore and ask questions about the materials they choose before using them in their pictures? Using magnifying glasses and information books, for example.

Questions for the children:

- How has your picture changed since you started it?

- What materials have you used?

- Where do you think each object has come from?

 "I don't want the pebbles here anymore, I need to get some grass instead."

How does the activity enable children to develop and demonstrate the characteristics of effective learning?

Characteristic of effective learning	The enabling environment: Transient art
Playing and exploring – engagement ● Finding out and exploring. ● Playing with what they know. ● Being willing to 'have a go'.	Some of the natural materials will be familiar others will be new and intriguing. Children can self-select the materials and resources they want to use.
Active learning – motivation ● Being involved and concentrating. ● Keeping trying. ● Enjoying achieving what they set out to do.	With no end product and an abundance of materials to work with, the opportunities for creativity are endless.
Creating and thinking critically – thinking ● Having their own ideas. ● Making links. ● Choosing ways to do things.	Children have the opportunity to understand that the non-permanent nature of their creations allows them to make changes to their work however and whenever they choose. Children can express their own ideas freely and choose exactly how they want to do something, reworking and adapting their work without the pressure of an end product.

Bespoke framing

Natural painting tools

Chapter Two: Fine motor skills

Key Areas of EYFS developed in this chapter:

- Physical Development

- Literacy

- Mathematics

- Expressive Arts and Design.

Activities for this chapter are:

- Feed me
- Snow write
- Colander thread
- A brush with nature
- Pom pom sort
- Peg it
- Wonder webs.

Useful resources for activities in this chapter:

- Tennis balls
- Small gems, beads, buttons, pom poms
- Clothes pegs
- Lolly sticks
- Sticks, plants and leaves
- Paint brushes
- Tweezers
- String.

Getting the muscles in the hand coordinated and strong enough to perform precise and refined movements is essential if children are to confidently and independently access the word around them. Hand-eye coordination, body awareness, bi-lateral coordination, hand and finger strength and hand dominance and are some of the factors central to the development of fine motor skills and support children to:

- Carry out every day self-care tasks such as dressing and feeding themselves.
- Play and interact with others.
- Engage in academic activities such as writing, drawing, painting, cutting and using computers.

Fine motor activities that allow children to grasp, pinch, poke, manipulate, pick up and release are not only central to their physical development but can simultaneously support and enhance their development across the other areas of learning. Literacy, specifically writing, is just one area that benefits enormously from these opportunities.

Examples of how fine motor activities can support the development of other areas of learning:

- **Communication and Language: Listening and attention** can be developed through fine motor activities that require children to concentrate for sustained periods of time. When threading for example or when using tools such as tweezers that require careful precision.
- **Numeracy** can be developed through fine motor activities that require children to sort, count, match and problem solve.
- **Expressive Arts and Design: Exploring and using media and materials** can be developed through fine motor activities that require children to paint using small and unusual tools.

Poor fine motor skills can have serious implications on children's overall development. Behaviour, engagement and self-confidence can all suffer as children become frustrated. Similarly, academic performance can suffer if children are unable to meet the expected standards in writing or don't have the skills required to interact with IT equipment. It is therefore vital to keep children motivated by providing a range of interesting and engaging fine motor activities.

You will find specific links and resources for each activity in this chapter.

Getting to grips with tricky tools

A tennis ball creature provides a fun exercise to strengthen little hands

Feed me

 "I fed him 4 gems because
that is how old I am."

Setting up the provision

Method

Using a craft knife make a slit in a tennis ball to form a
mouth. Draw on a pair of eyes with a marker and you
have a creature ready to squeeze for feeding. Provide a
selection of small objects for children to feed the tennis
ball. Plastic gems, beads and buttons will all work well.

Resources

- Tennis ball
- Craft knife
- Marker pen
- Plastic gems
- Small beads
- Buttons.

Handy hints

- Add letters to the 'food' and challenge the children to
  feed the creature to spell out simple words or their name.

- Add numbers to the 'food' and challenge the children
  to feed the creature the numbers in the correct order
  or to feed it the correct answer to a simple sum.

- Once the mouth has been made, encourage the
  children to decorate their creature with felt tip pens
  and craft materials, creating their own creatures to
  take home and feed.

- Challenge children to work in pairs to use a spoon to
  feed their creature.

How does the activity enable children to develop and demonstrate the characteristics of effective learning?

Characteristic of effective learning	The enabling environment: Feed me
Playing and exploring – engagement ● Finding out and exploring. ● Playing with what they know. ● Being willing to 'have a go'.	Colourful and glistening resources will draw children to the activity. Children have the opportunity to seek challenge.
Active learning – motivation ● Being involved and concentrating. ● Keeping trying. ● Enjoying achieving what they set out to do.	Children will need to persevere to successfully squeeze open the tennis ball. The activity requires careful concentration and precision.
Creating and thinking critically – thinking ● Having their own ideas. ● Making links. ● Choosing ways to do things.	Children can discover for themselves the best way to use the equipment. Children can set their own challenges and try to improve on what they have achieved previously.

Colourful and inviting

How the activity can support children's development across the 7 areas of learning

Areas of Learning: Personal, Social and Emotional Development

Children have the opportunity to:
- Challenge themselves.
- Maintain attention.

Areas of Learning: Communication and Language

Children have the opportunity to:
- Describe how to use the resources.
- Follow simple instructions.
- Explain the rules to any challenges they set.

Areas of Learning: Physical Development

Children have the opportunity to:
- Build the strength in their hands.
- Develop their bilateral motor coordination.
- Develop hand eye coordination.
- Develop their pincer grip.

Areas of Learning: Literacy

Children have the opportunity to:
- Spell simple words.
- Spell their name.
- Order letters alphabetically.

Areas of Learning: Mathematics

Children have the opportunity to:
- Order numbers.
- Count.
- Sort the gems by colour.
- Measure short periods of time.

Areas of Learning: Understanding the World

Children have the opportunity to:
- Investigate the use of force on an object.

Areas of Learning: Expressive Arts and Design

Children have the opportunity to:
- Design, draw and decorate.

Questions to help you extend the activity and to ensure challenge

Questions for you:
- Are sand timers or stop watches available for children to set their own timed challenges?

- Are resources available for children to record their scores and the words they make?

Questions for the children:
- How many gems can you feed your creature before the sand timer runs out?

- Is it easier to open the creature's mouth when you squeeze it with your left hand or your right hand?

- Can you feed your creature the letters in your name?

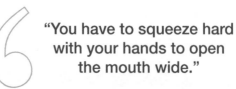

"You have to squeeze hard with your hands to open the mouth wide."

Success requires careful concentration

Using nature's blank canvas

Snow write

Setting up the provision

Method
Make the most of the cold weather, take paintbrushes and pots of water outside so that the children have the opportunity to write/mark make in the frost or snow. Encourage children to explore different surfaces, making marks wherever the snow has settled.

Resources
- Frost/Snow
- Pots of water
- Paintbrushes.

Handy hints
- Adapt your planning. Seize the opportunity to explore the snow while you can.

"You need to write quick before it all melts."

- Encourage children to explore the effects of a range of mark making tools in the snow. Glue spatulas, toy cars and sticks for example.

- Gather snow for use inside. Place it in a builder's tray or a water tray and use it as part of a small world scene.

Questions to help you extend the activity and to ensure challenge

Questions for you:
- Are there opportunities for children to revisit their marks later in the day to observe any changes?

- What will they notice?

How the activity can support children's development across the 7 areas of learning

Areas of Learning: Personal, Social and Emotional Development

Children have the opportunity to:
- Share resources.
- Seek delight in new experiences.

Areas of Learning: Communication and Language

Children have the opportunity to:
- Develop their vocabulary being introduced to key words such as *freeze, melt, weather, temperature, change.*

Areas of Learning: Physical Development

Children have the opportunity to:
- Develop control over a range of mark making and writing tools.

Areas of Learning: Literacy

Children have the opportunity to:
- Mark make.
- Write own name and simple words.
- Practise letter formation.

Areas of Learning: Mathematics

Children have the opportunity to:
- Practise number formation.

Areas of Learning: Understanding the World

Children have the opportunity to:
- Observe and comment on the changing weather.
- Explore freezing and melting.

Areas of Learning: Expressive Arts and Design

Children have the opportunity to:
- Experiment with pattern making.
- Make simple representations of objects and people.

Writing a secret ice code

- Once the snow has melted could you provide opportunities for mark making in other white materials? Shaving foam, flour, glue, oats or white paint for example.

- Are letters and numbers displayed clearly outside as well as inside?

Questions for the children:
- How does it feel as you are writing?

- What has happened to the marks that you made earlier?

 "I have written my sister's name in the snow."

 "You can use a stick for a pencil."

How does the activity enable children to develop and demonstrate the characteristics of effective learning?

Characteristic of effective learning	The enabling environment: Snow write
Playing and exploring – engagement ● Finding out and exploring. ● Playing with what they know. ● Being willing to 'have a go'.	Children have the opportunity to investigate something completely new, exploring the effects of the cold weather.
Active learning – motivation ● Being involved and concentrating. ● Keeping trying. ● Enjoying achieving what they set out to do.	Children can enjoy writing and mark making in a new way, using a range of tools. Children can take satisfaction from engaging in mark making on a large scale.
Creating and thinking critically – thinking ● Having their own ideas. ● Making links. ● Choosing ways to do things.	Children can express their own opinions, deciding which tools are the easiest/most pleasing to use and explaining why.

Once the snow has melted outside, replicate it inside.

New uses for household objects.

Colander thread

 "It is quite tricky
for my fingers."

Setting up the provision

Method

Provide colanders and a selection of pipe cleaners for children to thread through the holes. Coloured beads can also be added to their designs.

Resources

- Colander
- Pipe cleaners
- Beads.

Handy hints

- The coloured beads could be used to create repeating patterns.
- Add numbers to the beads for ordering or add letters to the beads for children to make simple words.

- Replace the pipe cleaners with real or artificial flowers for a spot of flower arranging!

Questions to help you extend the activity and to ensure challenge

Questions for you:

- Could you provide paper and coloured pens for children to record the patterns they make with their beads?

- Are there opportunities for children to write down the words they make?

- Could the decorated colanders be used as role play props?

How does the activity enable children to develop and demonstrate the characteristics of effective learning?

Characteristic of effective learning	The enabling environment: Colander thread
Playing and exploring – engagement ● Finding out and exploring. ● Playing with what they know. ● Being willing to 'have a go'.	Children have the opportunity to seek challenge. The activity promotes curiosity. What are the objects and how they are to be used together?
Active learning – motivation ● Being involved and concentrating. ● Keeping trying. ● Enjoying achieving what they set out to do.	The activity requires high levels of concentration. Children have the opportunity to persevere with a challenging technique.
Creating and thinking critically – thinking ● Having their own ideas. ● Making links. ● Choosing ways to do things.	Children can work out the best way of using the equipment, trying out different techniques and collaborating with others for support.

Such Focus

How the activity can support children's development across the 7 areas of learning

Areas of Learning: Personal, Social and Emotional Development
Children have the opportunity to:
- Ask for help when needed.
- Persevere when learning a new technique.

Areas of Learning: Communication and Language
Children have the opportunity to:
- Talk through what they are doing as they do it.
- Listen to and follow instructions.

Areas of Learning: Physical Development
Children have the opportunity to:
- Build the strength in their hands.
- Develop their bilateral motor coordination.
- Develop hand eye coordination.
- Develop their pincer grip.

Areas of Learning: Literacy
Children have the opportunity to:
- Read and spell simple words.

Areas of Learning: Mathematics
Children have the opportunity to:
- Make and record repeating patterns.
- Order numbers.

Areas of Learning: Understanding the World
Children have the opportunity to:
- Discover how things works.

Areas of Learning: Expressive Arts and Design
Children have the opportunity to:
- Make and record colour patterns.
- Design and decorate.

Questions for the children:
- Can you describe your bead pattern?
- What is the best way to thread the pipe cleaners through the holes?

"You need to push it through and then turn it over to find the other end."

"If you fold over the end it stops it from coming out of the hole."

A fiddly task for a young florist

A rustic alternative to your ordinary paint brush

A brush with nature

Targeted areas of learning:
Physical Development and Expressive
Arts and Design

 "This makes a
spiky dot pattern."

Setting up the provision

Method

Attach leaves, fir cones, feathers and other light weight
natural objects to strong sticks, using string, pegs or
elastic bands. Dip your natural brush into paint and
explore the effects.

Resources

- Sticks
- Natural objects such as feather, leaves, fir cones and
  grass
- String or elastic bands
- Paint
- Plain paper
- Clothes pegs.

Handy hints

- Swap the sticks for clothes pegs, making it easier
  for children to create their own paintbrushes
  independently.

- The stalks of some large leaves, such as rhubarb, may
  provide their own useful handles.

Questions to help you extend the activity and to ensure challenge

Questions for you:

- After exploring the brushes that have already been
  made, are there opportunities for children to gather
  resources to make their own peg paintbrushes?

How the activity can support children's development across the 7 areas of learning

Areas of Learning: Personal, Social and Emotional Development

Children have the opportunity to:
- Respond to simple instructions.
- Ask questions about the natural materials they are using.

Areas of Learning: Communication and language

Children have the opportunity to:
- Express their own opinions, deciding and explaining which materials they enjoy using and why.

Areas of Learning: Physical Development

Children have the opportunity to:
- Develop their pincer grip using the pegs.
- Develop the strength in their hands.

Areas of Learning: Literacy

Children have the opportunity to:
- Create story settings.

Areas of Learning: Mathematics

Children have the opportunity to:
- Identify and describe shapes and patterns.

Areas of Learning: Understanding of the World

Children have the opportunity to:
- Observe and comment on features of natural objects.
- Use tools for a specific purpose.

Areas of Learning: Expressive Arts and Design

Children have the opportunity to:
- Combine different media to create new effects.
- Discuss the effects of different tools, commenting on patterns, shapes and sounds.
- Use tools and techniques to assemble and join materials.

A pleasing swish, swash sound

- Is key vocabulary displayed to help children to describe the effects of their brushes?

Questions for the children:
- Which paint brush did you enjoy using the most?

- Can you talk about the patterns that you have made?

- What else could we use as a paintbrush?

 "It's nice and smooth. I can make the waves in the sea."

 "It's such a messy brush."

How does the activity enable children to develop and demonstrate the characteristics of effective learning?

Characteristic of effective learning	The enabling environment: A brush with nature
Playing and exploring – engagement ● Finding out and exploring. ● Playing with what they know. ● Being willing to 'have a go'.	The activity is multi-sensory. Children can use familiar objects in new ways. Children have the opportunity to explore and investigate objects that are unfamiliar.
Active learning – motivation ● Being involved and concentrating. ● Keeping trying. ● Enjoying achieving what they set out to do.	Children have the opportunity to persevere when using tools and learning new techniques. Assembling the brushes requires careful concentration.
Creating and thinking critically – thinking ● Having their own ideas. ● Making links. ● Choosing ways to do things.	Children can experiment with the effects of the different brushes, deciding how they should be used and deciding which they prefer.

Brushes that change with the seasons

Sort the pom-poms into the right colour pot

CHALLENGE
Can you count how many there are in each pot?

Simple but effective

Pom pom sort

 "Quick, get all of the blue ones first before we run out of time."

Setting up the provision

Method

Set up a bright and colourful area that will catch children's attention and encourage them to come and try the activity.

Provide a selection of bowls in colours that match your pom poms and pairs of tweezers. Set challenges such as sorting by colour, collecting a given amount or racing against a timer.

Resources

- Pom poms or small counters
- Tweezers/tongs
- Coloured pots
- Sand timer.

Handy hints

- Add a whiteboard or recordable talking button for setting daily challenges.

- Add letters to the pom poms or counters so that they can be sorted into the pot displaying the matching letter.

Questions to help you extend the activity and to ensure challenge

Questions for you:

- How could you incorporate challenges to help support wider literacy and mathematics in addition to developing the children's fine motor skills?

- Are there differentiated challenges?

How does the activity enable children to develop and demonstrate the characteristics of effective learning?

Characteristic of effective learning	The enabling environment: Pom pom sort
Playing and exploring – engagement ● Finding out and exploring. ● Playing with what they know. ● Being willing to 'have a go'.	Colourful resources will help draw children to the activity. Children have the opportunity to seek challenge.
Active learning – motivation ● Being involved and concentrating. ● Keeping trying. ● Enjoying achieving what they set out to do.	Children will need to persevere to successfully use the tweezers. The activity requires careful concentration.
Creating and thinking critically – thinking ● Having their own ideas. ● Making links. ● Choosing ways to do things.	Children can set their own challenges and try to improve on what they have achieved previously.

Precision is key

How the activity can support children's development across the 7 areas of learning

Areas of Learning: Personal, Social and Emotional Development

Children have the opportunity to:
- Share resources.
- Seek delight in challenging themselves.

Areas of Learning: Communication and Language

Children have the opportunity to:
- Describe how to use the resources.
- Follow simple instructions.
- Explain the rules to any challenges they set.

Areas of Learning: Physical Development

Children have the opportunity to:
- Develop their pincer grip.
- Develop the strength in their hands.
- Develop hand eye coordination.

Areas of Learning: Literacy

Children have the opportunity to:
- Match and sort letters.

Areas of Learning: Mathematics

Children have the opportunity to:
- Count.
- Sort by colour.
- Compare quantities.
- Add two groups of objects together.
- Share objects in equal groups.

Areas of Learning: Understanding the World

Children have the opportunity to:
- Discover how tools work.

Areas of Learning: Expressive Arts and Design

Children have the opportunity to:
- Identify and match colours.

- Can you challenge children to use the tweezers with their non-dominant hand?

Questions for the children:
- Can you share the pom poms equally between all of the pots?

- How many pom poms do you think you will be able to pick up before the sand timer runs out?

- Can you explain how to use the tweezers?

"There are 4 pom poms in the red pot and only 2 in the purple pot."

"You have to push your fingers together to use the tweezers."

A race against the sand timer!

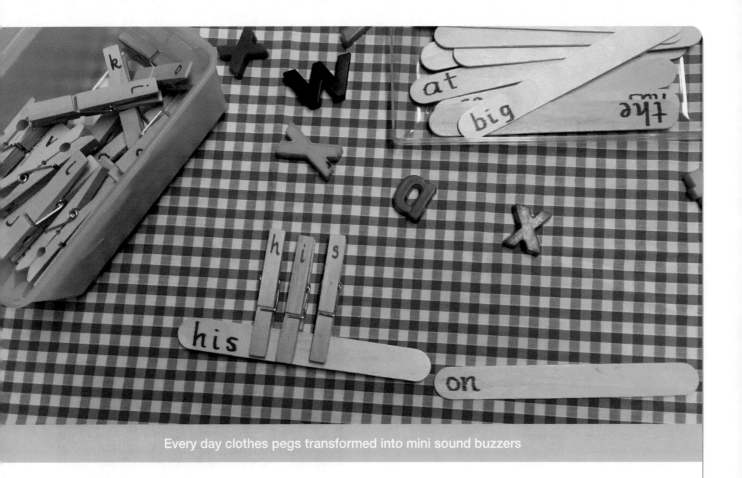

Every day clothes pegs transformed into mini sound buzzers

Peg it

Targeted areas of learning:
Physical Development and Literacy

 "I've made 5 words."

Setting up the provision

Method
Make a collection of pegs with letters written on them and a collection of lolly sticks with words on. Support children to hunt for the letters needed to spell out the words and then to peg them onto their word stick in the correct order.

Resources
- Lolly sticks
- Clothes pegs
- Marker pen.

Handy hints
- The activity could be used for self-registration. Each child finds the lolly stick with their name on and then pegs on each letter in turn.

- Utilise branches outside or clothes hangers to peg the alphabet.

- Swap the words for numbers so that children can attach the corresponding number of pegs to numeral.

Questions to help you extend the activity and to ensure challenge

Questions for you
- Could you provide blank sticks so that children can peg their own words prompted by picture cards?

- Are there opportunities for children to write down the words they have pegged?

How the activity can support children's development across the 7 areas of learning

Areas of Learning: Personal, Social and Emotional Development

Children have the opportunity to:

- Seek delight in challenging themselves.

Areas of Learning: Communication and Language

Children have the opportunity to:

- Maintain attention.

Areas of Learning: Physical Development

Children have the opportunity to:

- Develop the strength in their hands.
- Develop their pincer grip.

Areas of Learning: Literacy

Children have the opportunity to:

- Practise blending and segmenting to read and write simple words.
- Recognise and write their own name.

Areas of Learning: Mathematics

Children have the opportunity to:

- Count and compare the number of letters in different words and names.
- Swap the words for numbers and match quantity to numeral.

Areas of Learning: Understanding the World

Children have the opportunity to:

- Discover new ways to use familiar objects.

Areas of Learning: Expressive Arts and Design

Children have the opportunity to:

- Draw pictures to match the words they have pegged.

Smaller pegs but a bigger challenge

Questions for the children

- Can you read the word on your stick by sounding out each peg as you clip it on?

- Can you choose a picture card and find the correct pegs to make that word?

"It will take so long to peg my name because it's got 7 letters in it."

"My fingers are being a crocodile's mouth."

How does the activity enable children to develop and demonstrate the characteristics of effective learning?

Characteristic of effective learning	The enabling environment: Peg it
Playing and exploring – engagement ● Finding out and exploring. ● Playing with what they know. ● Being willing to 'have a go'.	Children can investigate the resources and discover for themselves how the activity works.
Active learning – motivation ● Being involved and concentrating. ● Keeping trying. ● Enjoying achieving what they set out to do.	Children have the opportunity to challenge themselves. Children have the opportunity to persevere using the resources.
Creating and thinking critically – thinking ● Having their own ideas. ● Making links. ● Choosing ways to do things.	Children have the opportunity to develop and extend the activity.

Sounding out the word one peg at a time

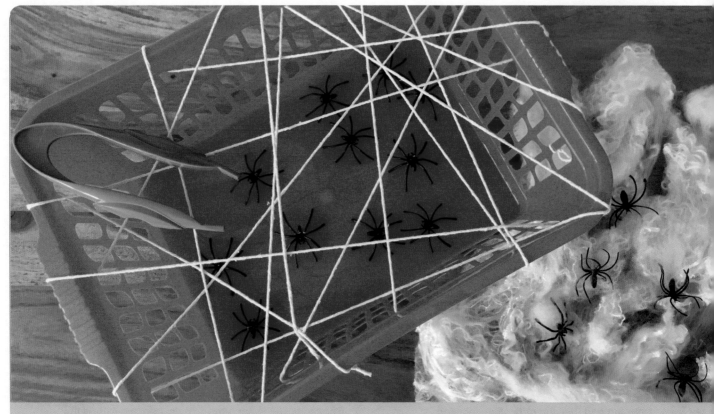

Carefully negotiate the web to capture the spiders.

Wonder webs

"You have to be careful
so that you don't get tangled
in the web."

Setting up the provision

Method

Place a handful of plastic spiders at the bottom of a
basket with holes in the side. Support children to thread
string through the holes in their basket, weaving back and
forth to create a web effect. Provide tweezers, tongs and
clothes peg for collecting the spiders.

Resources

- Plastic basket with holes in the side
- String or white wool
- Plastic spiders
- Tweezers/tongs or clothes pegs
- Spaghetti
- Food colouring.

Handy hints

- The more string you use, the smaller the gaps and the
  harder it becomes!

- Add numbers to the spiders so that they can be
  collected in numerical order.

- Add letters to the spiders so that they can be collected
  in alphabetical order.

- Arrange the spiders to spell out simple words.

- Make webs on other materials, such as leaves, paper
  plates or black card, using just a hole punch and string.

How does the activity enable children to develop and demonstrate the characteristics of effective learning?

Characteristic of effective learning	The enabling environment: Wonder webs
Playing and exploring – engagement ● Finding out and exploring. ● Playing with what they know. ● Being willing to 'have a go'.	Children have the opportunity to seek challenge.
Active learning – motivation ● Being involved and concentrating. ● Keeping trying. ● Enjoying achieving what they set out to do.	The activity requires high levels of concentration. Children have the opportunity to persevere when using the resources. Children can compete against themselves and each other.
Creating and thinking critically – thinking ● Having their own ideas. ● Making links. ● Choosing ways to do things.	Children have the opportunity to make links with familiar stories, songs and rhymes. Children can make comparisons with and talk about any real webs that they have seen. Children have the opportunity to use different tools, deciding which is the most effective.

Swap the basket and string for a vibrant web of dyed spaghetti.

How the activity can support children's development across the 7 areas of learning

Areas of Learning: Personal, Social and Emotional Development

Children have the opportunity to:
- Challenge themselves.

Areas of Learning: Communication and Language

Children have the opportunity to:
- Follow simple instructions.
- Main attention.

Areas of Learning: Physical Development

Children have the opportunity to:
- Build the strength in their hands.
- Develop their pincer grip.
- Develop hand eye coordination.

Areas of Learning: Literacy

Children have the opportunity to:
- Make links with familiar stories, songs and rhymes.
- Order letters alphabetically.

Areas of Learning: Mathematics

Children have the opportunity to:
- Count.
- Compare quantities.
- Add two groups of objects.
- Identify shapes made by the web.

Areas of Learning: Understanding the World

Children have the opportunity to:
- Make close observations of real spider webs.

Areas of Learning: Expressive Arts and Design

Children have the opportunity to:
- Explore pattern and shape.
- Use simple tools and techniques competently.

Questions to help you extend the activity and to ensure challenge

Questions for you:
- How are the tools for collecting the spiders differentiated? For some children just using their fingers will be challenging enough?

- Could children explore using rulers to draw their own spider's webs?

Questions for the children:
- Which tool is the easiest to use?

- Can you add up how many spiders you and your friend have collected altogether?

- What shapes can you see in the web?

"I have collected 6 spiders."

Which tool will provide the greatest challenge?

Realistic scenes

Chapter Three:
Small World

Key Areas of EYFS developed in this chapter:

- Communication and Language

- Understanding the World

- Expressive Arts and Design.

Activities for this chapter are:

- Vegetable forest
- Secret compartment
- Where 'shell' I hide
- Personal action figures

- The hole
- Down by the riverside
- Cereal construction.

Useful resources for activities in this chapter:

- Builder's tray, sand/water tray
- Assorted size rocks, sticks, stones, shells, logs and other interesting natural objects
- Flowers and plants
- Cereal
- Vegetables
- Clipboards and notebooks
- Plastic containers
- Coloured sand
- Paint

Chapter Three: Small world

- Play animals
- Play people.

Immersing themselves in their own small worlds enables children to share knowledge that they already have, whilst constantly learning and discovering new things. They have the opportunity to imagine, talk, listen, build friendships and problem solve. The potential small world play offers children's overall development is both exciting and invaluable.

A builder's tray or other shallow tray offers a flat and easily accessible surface, providing a good base for small world. However, there are many other ways to present your scenes. You may want to use:

- A flower pot
- A car tyre
- A suitcase
- Plants and bushes
- The base of a tree
- A hollowed out book
- A sand or water tray
- A bowl
- A shoe box

- A wheelbarrow
- A cup and saucer.

A whole new world of possibilities awaits.

You will find specific links and resources for each activity in this chapter.

Step inside your very own story

Edible resources

Vegetable forest

Targeted areas of learning:
Communication and Language and
Expressive Arts and Design

"This is the woods where
Grandma's cottage is."

Setting up the provision

Method

Arrange your chosen raw vegetables to make a forest
scene, placing play people and animals amongst broccoli
trees, potato rocks and salad grass. Provide extra
vegetables for children to select from so that they can
change and enhance the scene over time to suit the
stories that they want to tell.

Resources

- Raw Vegetables e.g. broccoli, cauliflower, potatoes
- Salad leaves
- Fresh herbs
- Play people
- Play animals.

Handy hints

- Use fresh herbs for the grass and foliage to stimulate
  children's sense of smell as they play and to help bring
  the scene to life.

- Swap broccoli trees for cauliflower trees for a change
  in weather conditions.

Questions to help you extend the activity and to ensure challenge

Questions for you

- Could you provide story books, illustrations and
  photographs of similar settings to help extend children's
  play and support their developing vocabulary?

How the activity can support children's development across the 7 areas of learning

Areas of Learning: Personal, Social and Emotional Development

Children have the opportunity to:
- Share resources.
- Play alongside other children engaged in the same theme.
- Keep play going by responding to what others say and do.

Areas of Learning: Communication and Language

Children have the opportunity to:
- Link statements and stick to a main theme as they talk.
- Use language to imagine and recreate roles and own experiences in play situations.
- Introduce a story line or narrative into their play.

Areas of Learning: Physical Development

Children have the opportunity to:
- Demonstrate control when handling small resources.
- Identify the different vegetables and talk about healthy eating.

Areas of Learning: Literacy

Children have the opportunity to:
- Retell familiar stories.
- Write their own stories.

Areas of Learning: Mathematics

Children have the opportunity to:
- Use everyday language related to time.

Areas of Learning: Understanding the World

Children have the opportunity to:
- Play with small world models.
- Share knowledge about their local environment and the natural world such as the weather and different habitats.

Areas of Learning: Expressive Arts and Design

Children have the opportunity to:
- Engage in imaginative play.
- Introduce a story line or narrative into their play.
- Explore and describe texture and smell.

Raid the fridge

- Are there opportunities for children to act out their small world stories on a larger scale with props and costumes/masks?

Questions for the children:
- Where in the world is this place?

- What animals might live here?

- What do you think the weather is like here?

 "I am using this blanket to make it dark so that we can pretend we are in a scary night time forest."

 "We might find the Gruffalo here."

How does the activity enable children to develop and demonstrate the characteristics of effective learning?

Characteristic of effective learning	The enabling environment: Vegetable forest
Playing and exploring – engagement ● Finding out and exploring. ● Playing with what they know. ● Being willing to 'have a go'.	The activity is open ended. It is likely that the children will be familiar with the vegetables and they will be excited to see them and use them in new ways. The familiar materials create opportunities for discussion and questions.
Active learning – motivation ● Being involved and concentrating. ● Keeping trying. ● Enjoying achieving what they set out to do.	Children have the opportunity to immerse themselves in a new world, acting out stories and maintaining their attention for a sustained period of time.
Creating and thinking critically – thinking ● Having their own ideas. ● Making links. ● Choosing ways to do things.	Being led by their imaginations, children can change the scene and the atmosphere. A calm and peaceful forest walk one minute, a terrifying bear hunt the next!

A feast for hungry bears

Secret compartment

Targeted areas of learning:
Communication and Language and
Literacy

Setting up the provision

Method

Draw a rectangle on the first page of a thick, hard back book, leaving a margin all the way around the edge. Using a craft knife and a metal ruler hollow out the inside to create a secret compartment to hide storytelling props of your choice. Leave the book for children to discover and support them to use the objects that they find inside to tell their own stories.

Resources

- Thick hard back book
- Craft Knife
- Metal ruler
- Small story telling props of your choice.

Handy hints

- Once you have made the resource it can be used over and over again.

- Simply change the objects inside and a whole new story is waiting to be told.

- You may want to start with a collection of objects from a story that the children are very familiar with before providing objects for them to make up their own new stories.

Questions to help you extend the activity and to ensure challenge

Questions for you

- Could children design a front cover for the book and come up with a title relevant to the objects they find inside?

- Are resources available for children to tell/write their own stories, inspired by what they find hiding in the secret compartment?

How does the activity enable children to develop and demonstrate the characteristics of effective learning?

Characteristic of effective learning	The enabling environment: Secret compartment
Playing and exploring – engagement ● Finding out and exploring. ● Playing with what they know. ● Being willing to 'have a go'.	The activity is open ended. The hidden compartment provides excitement and intrigue. Children have the opportunity to play with characters from familiar stories.
Active learning – motivation ● Being involved and concentrating. ● Keeping trying. ● Enjoying achieving what they set out to do.	The small hidden objects provide inspiration for storytelling and help to stimulate children's imaginations. Children have the opportunity to maintain their attention as they tell and act out their stories.
Creating and thinking critically – thinking ● Having their own ideas. ● Making links. ● Choosing ways to do things.	Children can make links with familiar stories, retelling them and creating their own versions. Children have the opportunity to create and develop their own characters.

Secret stories waiting to be told

How the activity can support children's development across the 7 areas of learning

Areas of Learning: Personal, Social and Emotional Development

Children have the opportunity to:

- Maintain attention.
- Have and share their own ideas.
- Keep play going by responding to what others say and do.

Areas of Learning: Communication and Language

Children have the opportunity to:

- Use language to imagine and recreate roles and own experiences in play situations.
- Link statements and stick to a main theme as they talk.
- Introduce a story line or narrative into their play.

Areas of Learning: Physical Development

Children have the opportunity to:

- Demonstrate control when handling small resources.

Areas of Learning: Literacy

Children have the opportunity to:

- Retell familiar stories.
- Develop an awareness of the way that stories are structured.
- Develop their own characters and settings.
- Suggest how a story might end.
- Use vocabulary and forms of speech in their play that are influenced by their experiences of books.

Areas of Learning: Mathematics

Children have the opportunity to:

- Use everyday language related to time.
- Sequence story events in the correct order.

Areas of Learning: Understanding the World

Children have the opportunity to:

- Play with small world models.

Areas of Learning: Expressive Arts and Design

Children have the opportunity to:

- Engage in imaginative play.
- Introduce a story line or narrative into their play.
- Build stories around toys and other objects.

Questions for the children

- What do you think happens when we close the book?
- Describe the characters in your story?
- Can you retell this story but make up a different ending?

 "The book is alive!"

 "When you shut the book, all the characters go to sleep."

"It's a magic book. The story is real."

Familiar characters hiding inside

Empty giant shells must mean that giant creatures are on the loose!

Where 'shell' I hide?

Targeted areas of learning:
Communication and Language and
Expressive Arts and Design

 "I have found the slime from a monster snail."

Setting up the provision

Method

Arrange a selection of large shells on the sand. Include as many interesting shapes, colours and textures as you can find. Position play people hiding, climbing or peering into them. Scatter plastic gems or other jewels all around with some placed inside the shells ready to be discovered. Leave the scene open for children to decide what has happened and to tell their own stories as they play.

Resources

- Assorted sized shells
- Play people
- Sand
- Gems/jewels.

Handy hints

- Play a real game of hide and seek.

- Hide some 'treasure' within your setting for your very own treasure hunt.

- Coloured sand in shakers allows you to add colourful designs and patterns to small world scenes.

Questions to help you extend the activity and to ensure challenge

Questions for you

- Could you provide resources for children to make their own treasure maps?

How the activity can support children's development across the 7 areas of learning

Areas of Learning: Personal, Social and Emotional Development

Children have the opportunity to:

- Share resources.
- Play alongside other children engaged in the same theme.
- Keep play going by responding to what others say and do.

Areas of Learning: Communication and Language

Children have the opportunity to:

- Use language to imagine and recreate roles and own experiences in play situations.
- Link statements and stick to a main theme as they talk.
- Introduce a story line or narrative into their play.

Areas of Learning: Physical Development

Children have the opportunity to:

- Demonstrate control when handling small resources.

Areas of Learning: Literacy

Children have the opportunity to:

- Write their own stories.
- Make links with familiar stories, songs and rhymes.
- Use vocabulary and forms of speech in their play that are influenced by their experiences of books.

Areas of Learning: Mathematics

Children have the opportunity to:

- Use everyday language related to time.
- Compare the size and shape and weight of the shells.

Areas of Learning: Understanding the World

Children have the opportunity to:

- Play with small world models.
- Share knowledge about their local environment and the natural world.

Areas of Learning: Expressive Arts and Design

Children have the opportunity to:

- Engage in imaginative play.
- Introduce a story line or narrative into their play.
- Build stories around toys and natural objects.

The creature has vanished but has left behind some precious jewels.

"This was where a hermit crab lived and now he has moved to a new shell house, maybe in Australia."

"Quick! We need to hide in case the giant crab comes back for his treasure."

- Could you extend your small world scene into a role play area?

- Could you provide information books or identification sheets to help children match and discover more about the shells?

Questions for the children

- What has happened here?

- Why are the shells empty?

- Which shell would you hide in?

How does the activity enable children to develop and demonstrate the characteristics of effective learning?

Characteristic of effective learning	The enabling environment: Where 'shell' I hide?
Playing and exploring – engagement ● Finding out and exploring. ● Playing with what they know. ● Being willing to 'have a go'.	The activity is open ended. Children have the opportunity to immerse themselves in imaginative play. Children have the opportunity to find out about the different shells, suggesting and questioning where they may have come from and what may have lived in them.
Active learning – motivation ● Being involved and concentrating. ● Keeping trying. ● Enjoying achieving what they set out to do.	The scene children are presented with is intriguing, helping to grab and hold their attention.
Creating and thinking critically – thinking ● Having their own ideas. ● Making links. ● Choosing ways to do things.	The objects provide a stimulus for children's imaginations. The scene is open for children to tell their own stories. Children can investigate the objects and discover new things for themselves.

A mysterious coloured trail. What could this mean?

Where in the world will you find yourself?

Personal action figures

Setting up the provision

Method

Take full length photographs of the children, print them out and then cut around the body. Laminate each photo for durability and attach them to a base. Wooden lolly sticks, cubes or small recycled containers such as yoghurt pots work well. Give each child their very own 'action figure' so that they can travel to new and mysterious lands.

Resources

- Camera
- Printer
- Laminator and laminating pouches
- Wooden lolly sticks, small cubes or small containers.

Handy hints

- Leave the figures hidden around the classroom for children to discover when they arrive!

- When making the figures you may want to include the practitioners in your setting and the children's parents.

- Use the action figures with small world activities, as an alternative to regular play people.

Questions to help you extend the activity and to ensure challenge

Questions for you

- Could you use this activity to support with transition and settling in periods?

- Could you set up a search activity where children have to find their friends' action figures hidden amongst the provision and mark off who they find using their own class registers?

How does the activity enable children to develop and demonstrate the characteristics of effective learning?

Characteristic of effective learning	The enabling environment: Personal action figures
Playing and exploring – engagement • Finding out and exploring. • Playing with what they know. • Being willing to 'have a go'.	The activity is open ended. The activity can help to develop children's confidence. Children can explore new areas of the setting through the security of their personalised figures.
Active learning – motivation • Being involved and concentrating. • Keeping trying. • Enjoying achieving what they set out to do.	The activity is enjoyable and amusing.
Creating and thinking critically – thinking • Having their own ideas. • Making links. • Choosing ways to do things.	Children have the opportunity to decide where in the world they want to travel to and who they want to take with them.

Be the main character in your own story

How the activity can support children's development across the 7 areas of learning

Areas of Learning: Personal, Social and Emotional Development

Children have the opportunity to:

- Demonstrate friendly behaviour.
- Show sensitivity to the needs and feelings of others.
- Keep play going by responding to what others say and do.
- Develop the confidence to explore new environments.

Areas of Learning: Communication and Language

Children have the opportunity to:

- Use vocabulary focused on objects and people that are of particular importance to them.
- Use language to imagine and recreate their own first hand experiences.
- Introduce a story line or narrative into their play.

Areas of Learning: Physical Development

Children have the opportunity to:

- Demonstrate control when handling small resources.

Areas of Learning: Literacy

Children have the opportunity to:

- Write their own stories, using themselves and their friends and family as the main characters.

Areas of Learning: Mathematics

Children have the opportunity to:

- Use everyday language related to time.
- Compare the size of the things around them in relation to their action figures.

Areas of Learning: Understanding the World

Children have the opportunity to:

- Share knowledge about their local environment and the natural world.
- Show an interest in different occupations.
- Make maps.

Areas of Learning: Expressive Arts and Design

Children have the opportunity to:

- Engage in imaginative play based on own first-hand experiences.
- Introduce a story line or narrative into their play.

Questions for the children

- Where have you travelled to?
- Where would you like to go next?
- Can you find any of your friends hidden outside?

> "I'm lost in the jungle, help!"

> "Look! It's little me and little you. That is so funny."

> "We are as tiny as the flowers."

Building friendships

A safari on your doorstep.

The hole

Targeted areas of learning: Communication and Language and Understanding the World

Setting up the provision

Method

Support the children to dig a small hole in a suitable patch of ground, big enough to place a plastic container. Fill the container with water and add your chosen small world animals. Create a scene around the outside of the 'hole' to bring your chosen environment to life, using the materials that are freely available such as the spare soil from the hole, sand, stones and plants.

Resources

- Plastic container
- Water
- Small world animals
- Natural materials such as sand, stone, plants and logs.

Handy hints

- By changing just a few resources you can create a brand new scene. Garden pond to dinosaur swap, lake to swimming pool... the possibilities are endless.

- Whisk up a squirt of washing up liquid to create an intriguing bubbling swamp.

- Mix a drop of food colouring or paint into the water to make the hole more vibrant and enticing.

Questions to help you extend the activity and to ensure challenge

Questions for you:

- Are resources available for children to self-select from so that they can adapt and transform their chosen environment?

- Are there books about habitats available to support and extend children's play?

How the activity can support children's development across the 7 areas of learning

Areas of Learning: Personal, Social and Emotional Development

Children have the opportunity to:
- Share resources.
- Play alongside other children engaged in the same theme.
- Keep play going by responding to what others say and do.

Areas of Learning: Communication and Language

Children have the opportunity to:
- Develop their vocabulary being introduced to key words such as *habitat, environment, mammal, reptile*.
- Use language to imagine and recreate their own first hand experiences.
- Introduce a story line or narrative into their play.

Areas of Learning: Physical Development

Children have the opportunity to:
- Demonstrate control when handling small resources.
- Develop their gross motor skills through digging.

Areas of Learning: Literacy

Children have the opportunity to:
- Write their own stories.
- Make links with familiar stories and songs.
- Explore non-fiction books.

Areas of Learning: Mathematics

Children have the opportunity to:
- Compare size and shape.
- Explore capacity.

Areas of Learning: Understanding the World

Children have the opportunity to:
- Play with small world models.
- Share knowledge about their local environment and the natural world. For example, knowledge about different animals and their habitats.

Areas of Learning: Expressive Arts and Design

Children have the opportunity to:
- Engage in imaginative play.
- Introduce a story line or narrative into their play.

Thirsty work

Questions for the children:
- How would we travel to this place?

- How could you sort these animals?

- What would you like to turn this hole into?

  "Let's get some sharks and turn it into the sea."

  "It is so hot in Africa, the animals need a nice cool drink."

  "All of these animals having a drink are mammals."

How does the activity enable children to develop and demonstrate the characteristics of effective learning?

Characteristic of effective learning	The enabling environment: The hole
Playing and exploring – engagement ● Finding out and exploring. ● Playing with what they know. ● Being willing to 'have a go'.	The activity is open ended. Children have the opportunity to play with familiar animals and find out about those that are less familiar.
Active learning – motivation ● Being involved and concentrating. ● Keeping trying. ● Enjoying achieving what they set out to do.	Children have the opportunity to immerse themselves in and create new worlds. They have the opportunity to act out their own stories, maintaining their attention for a sustained period of time.
Creating and thinking critically – thinking ● Having their own ideas. ● Making links. ● Choosing ways to do things.	Being led by their imaginations, children can change the scene, selecting from the available resources. Children have the opportunity to draw on their own knowledge when creating new environments for their animals.

Bubble wrap frogspawn to enhance a garden pond

Watch out for the crocs

Down by the riverside

Targeted areas of learning:
Communication and Language and
Understanding the World

Setting up the provision

Method

Create a river flowing through the middle of a sand tray by supporting children to dig a narrow trench from one end to the other. Mix some water with blue food colouring or paint and then pour it into the foil. Arrange crocodiles and trees along the banks of your river.

Resources

- Sand tray
- Aluminum foil
- Water
- Blue paint or food colouring
- Branches and small logs
- Pebbles and rocks
- Play crocodiles
- Play people.

Handy hints

- Provide pebbles for stepping stones and branches/ logs for building bridges.

- Plant stems and leaves can be pushed into the sand to make trees along the river bank.

- Display images of rivers from around the world to further support children's discussions and understanding.

Questions to help you extend the activity and to ensure challenge

Questions for you:

- Are there opportunities for problem solving? Making and testing bridges for example.

- Are there opportunities for children to learn about reflections?

How does the activity enable children to develop and demonstrate the characteristics of effective learning?

Characteristic of effective learning	The enabling environment: Down by the riverside
Playing and exploring – engagement ● Finding out and exploring. ● Playing with what they know. ● Being willing to 'have a go'.	The activity is open ended. Children have the opportunity to mix sand and water play. Children can use information books and images to help extend their knowledge as they play.
Active learning – motivation ● Being involved and concentrating. ● Keeping trying. ● Enjoying achieving what they set out to do.	Children have the opportunity to immerse themselves in a new world. They have the opportunity to act out their own stories, maintaining their attention for a sustained period of time.
Creating and thinking critically – thinking ● Having their own ideas. ● Making links. ● Choosing ways to do things.	Children have the opportunity to problem solve and investigate the effectiveness of different resources and materials when making bridges. Children can draw on their own experiences of rivers or other bodies of water as they play and investigate.

Do you dare to cross?

How the activity can support children's development across the 7 areas of learning

Areas of Learning: Personal, Social and Emotional Development

Children have the opportunity to:

- Maintain attention.
- Share resources.
- Play alongside other children engaged in the same theme.
- Keep play going by responding to what other say and do.

Areas of Learning: Communication and Language

Children have the opportunity to:

- Use language to imagine and recreate their own first hand experiences.
- Link statements and stick to a main theme as they talk.
- Introduce a story line or narrative into their play.

Areas of Learning: Physical Development

Children have the opportunity to:

- Demonstrate control when handling small resources.

Areas of Learning: Literacy

Children have the opportunity to:

- Write their own stories.
- Make links with familiar stories and songs.
- Use vocabulary and forms of speech in their play that are influenced by their experiences of books.
- Read non-fiction books.

Areas of Learning: Mathematics

Children have the opportunity to:

- Investigate weight and length.
- Explore capacity.

Areas of Learning: Understanding the World

Children have the opportunity to:

- Play with small world models.
- Share knowledge about their local environment and the natural world.

Areas of Learning: Expressive Arts and Design

Children have the opportunity to:

- Engage in imaginative play.
- Introduce a story line or narrative into their play.

- Could you provide further opportunities for children to investigate flowing water? Creating a water wall for example, using old bottles, funnels, pipes, jugs and watering cans.

Questions for the children

- How could you get across the river safely?

- Do you know the names of any rivers?

- What stories do you know where the characters have to cross a river?

"We need to build a bridge to stay safe from the crocodiles."

"You can make a strong bridge with metal."

Observing the reflections in the water

Building materials or breakfast?

Cereal construction

 **"I am using a bulldozer
to flatten everything."**

Setting up the provision

Method

Arrange your chosen breakfast cereal to make a
construction site scene, placing play people and trucks
amongst wheat biscuit bricks, cornflake gravel and
puffed rice rocks. Provide extra cereal for children to
select from so that they can replenish and adapt the
scene as they play.

Resources

- Builder's tray
- A variety of cereal
- Play trucks
- Play people
- Hazard tape.

Handy hints

- Add clipboards, measuring tapes, hard hats and high
  visibility jackets to enhance children's imaginative play.

- Provide cereal with many different textures and listen
  out for the sounds made as the trucks drive over them.

Questions to help you extend the activity and to ensure challenge

Questions for you:

- Could you encourage children to make their own site
  maps and building plans, using the clipboards?

- Could you support name writing by encouraging children
  to sign their name on a 'worker's register' before playing?

How the activity can support children's development across the 7 areas of learning

Areas of Learning: Personal, Social and Emotional Development

Children have the opportunity to:

- Maintain attention.
- Share resources.
- Play alongside other children engaged in the same theme.

Areas of Learning: Communication and Language

Children have the opportunity to:

- Use language to imagine and recreate their own first hand experiences.
- Link statements and stick to a main theme as they talk.
- Introduce a story line or narrative into their play.

Areas of Learning: Physical Development

Children have the opportunity to:

- Demonstrate control when handling small resources.

Areas of Learning: Literacy

Children have the opportunity to:

- Design and label their own buildings.
- Practise name writing.
- Write a list of materials and tools required.

Areas of Learning: Mathematics

Children have the opportunity to:

- Compare and talk about shape, size and weight.
- Explore measuring tapes, rulers and non-standard measurement.

Areas of Learning: Understanding the World

Children have the opportunity to:

- Play with small world models.
- Share knowledge about their local environment and the natural world.
- Show an interest in different occupations.

Areas of Learning: Expressive Arts and Design

Children have the opportunity to:

- Engage in imaginative play.
- Introduce a story line or narrative into their play.
- Build stories around toys.

Inspired by the surrounding architecture

Questions for the children:

- What are you building or demolishing?

- Tell me about your building materials

- What tools do you need?

 "I am scooping up sand and bricks to build my flat."

"Let's build a tower with 100 floors."

How does the activity enable children to develop and demonstrate the characteristics of effective learning?

Characteristic of effective learning	The enabling environment: Cereal construction
Playing and exploring – engagement ● Finding out and exploring. ● Playing with what they know. ● Being willing to 'have a go'.	The activity is open ended. It is likely that the children will be familiar with the cereal and they will be excited to see and use it in new ways. The familiar materials create opportunities for discussion and questions.
Active learning – motivation ● Being involved and concentrating. ● Keeping trying. ● Enjoying achieving what they set out to do.	Children have the opportunity to immerse themselves in a new world and occupation. They have the opportunity to act out their own stories, maintaining their attention for a sustained period of time.
Creating and thinking critically – thinking ● Having their own ideas. ● Making links. ● Choosing ways to do things.	Children can use the buildings and architecture in the environment around them to support and extend their play. Children have the opportunity to design their own buildings and decide how to build them.

Under construction

Busy fingers

Chapter Four: Creativity

Key areas of EYFS developed in this chapter:

- Physical Development

- Understanding the World

- Expressive Arts and Design.

Activities for this chapter are:

- Painted toast
- Window art
- Ice paint
- Coffee break
- Recipe challenge
- Spice it up
- How handy.

Useful resources for activities in this chapter:

- Paint and paint brushes
- Food colouring
- Water
- Collage materials
- Sand
- Herbs and spices
- A variety of uncooked long life food such as dried pasta, rice and lentils
- Assorted cooking utensils.

Encouraging children to enjoy the experience itself rather than striving for a particular end product is at the heart of creativity in the early years. Creativity is not something that can be confined to a designated 'art area'. Instead opportunities for creative thinking and learning should be all around. Activities ought not to be prescriptive but open-ended and should actively engage children's imaginations.

They should be able to freely communicate their ideas, express their own opinions and be given time to reflect.

Types of activity to support children's creativity could include:

- Role play
- Storytelling
- Painting and drawing
- Sculpting
- Music and dance
- Cooking.

This is by no means an exhaustive list.

When planning and resourcing these activities, thinking beyond the ordinary will help to engage children.

Ask yourself:
- What could children use to paint with besides paintbrushes?
- Could the activity be replicated or enhanced on a larger scale outside?
- What malleable materials could children use for their sculptures?

- How could you make the activity multi sensory?
- What interesting surfaces could children use?

Fundamental to children's developing creativity is the opportunity to play and the chance to choose how to do things for themselves. As adults we can provide children with the resources and starting points. We can ask open-ended questions, model creative behaviours and praise original ideas. With no predetermined expectation of how children's work should look or how they should approach a particular task, the focus remains very much on the process itself with the children leading the way.

You will find specific links and resources for each activity in this chapter.

There's no such thing as mess!

Turning milk into paint

Painted toast

Setting up the provision

Method

Fill small dishes with milk, and using a pipette, add a few drops of food colouring to each one. Support children to dip their paintbrushes into the coloured milk and to paint directly onto a slice of white bread. They can then toast their colourful slices.

Resources

- White bread
- Milk
- Food colouring
- Small dishes
- Paint brushes
- Toaster
- Pipettes.

Handy hints

- Thick cut bread provides a more stable base to paint on.

- Toast the bread and observe how the colour sets.

- Display children's individual slices altogether at the end of the session to make an edible patchwork.

Questions to help you extend the activity and to ensure challenge

Questions for you:

- Are there opportunities for children to use coloured pencils, pens or paints to design their bread paintings on paper first?

- Could you create an opportunity for children to develop fairy tales or adventure stories around their painted toast?

Questions for the children:

- Tell me about your painting.

How does the activity enable children to develop and demonstrate the characteristics of effective learning?

Characteristic of effective learning	The enabling environment: Painted toast
Playing and exploring – engagement ● Finding out and exploring. ● Playing with what they know. ● Being willing to 'have a go'.	The combination of materials provided is intriguing and exciting, encouraging children to try the activity. They will enjoy using familiar materials in a new way.
Active learning – motivation ● Being involved and concentrating. ● Keeping trying. ● Enjoying achieving what they set out to do.	Children have the opportunity to maintain their attention as they create their own designs and engage in a new and unusual experience. Children have the opportunity to see their finished art work displayed in a new way.
Creating and thinking critically – thinking ● Having their own ideas. ● Making links. ● Choosing ways to do things.	Children have the freedom to create their own paintings, selecting and mixing the colours they want to use and exploring different patterns and designs.

Your very own bread canvas

How the activity can support children's development across the 7 areas of learning

Areas of Learning: Personal, Social and Emotional Development

Children have the opportunity to:
- Develop the confidence to try new activities.
- Welcome and value praise.

Areas of Learning: Communication and Language

Children have the opportunity to:
- Maintain attention.
- Use talk to organise, sequence and clarify thinking, ideas, feelings and events.
- Questions why things happen and offer explanations.

Areas of Learning: Physical Development

Children have the opportunity to:
- Demonstrate control when using a paintbrush.

Areas of Learning: Literacy

Children have the opportunity to:
- Mark make.
- Write letters.
- Write own name.
- Give meanings to marks.

Areas of Learning: Mathematics

Children have the opportunity to:
- Write numbers.
- Paint and describe patterns and shapes.

Areas of Learning: Understanding the World

Children have the opportunity to:
- Explain and question why things happen and how things work.

Areas of Learning: Expressive Arts and Design

Children have the opportunity to:
- Understand that different media can be combined to create new effects.
- Choose particular colours to use for a purpose.
- Explore colour mixing.
- Create patterns and shapes.
- Make simple representations of people and objects.

- How does it feel as you paint on the bread?

- What exciting things might happen if you eat your colourful slice?

"This is rainbow bread for my fairy."

"I made circle and triangle shapes on my bread."

"It's squishy to paint on."

A potential story prop

Mixing water play and art

Window art

Setting up the provision

Method
Provide children with a selection of collage materials such as foam shapes, tissue paper, sequins and googly eyes. Support them to create pictures on an accessible window or glass door panel using water as their 'glue'.

Resources
- An accessible window or glass door panel
- Collage materials such as foam shapes, tissue paper, sequins and googly eyes
- Pot of water
- Paintbrushes
- A small towel or kitchen roll
- Plastc mirrors.

Handy hints
- The same activity can be replicated on a mirror.
- Fallen leaves stick well with water for an autumn art activity.
- Many of the materials will stick on top of each other enabling children to experiment with layering.

Questions to help you extend the activity and to ensure challenge

Questions for you:
- Are children able to use a variety of collage materials, testing out how they react with the water and deciding if they would make effective materials for the activity?
- When sticking collage materials onto a mirror, could children use their reflections to create self-portraits?
- Could you support children to take photos of their transient window pictures?

How the activity can support children's development across the 7 areas of learning

Areas of Learning: Personal, Social and Emotional Development

Children have the opportunity to:

- Have their own ideas and select materials and resources independently.
- Work on their own individual projects or collaboratively with others.

Areas of Learning: Communication and Language

Children have the opportunity to:

- Maintain attention.
- Talk through what they are doing, organising and clarifying their ideas.

Areas of Learning: Physical Development

Children have the opportunity to:

- Handle and arrange small materials with control and purpose.
- Demonstrate control using a paintbrush.

Areas of Learning: Literacy

Children have the opportunity to:

- Create letters.
- Spell out words.

Areas of Learning: Mathematics

Children have the opportunity to:

- Make repeating patterns.
- Identify and describe 2D shapes.

Areas of Learning: Understanding the World

Children have the opportunity to:

- Describe patterns.
- Observe changes over time.
- Use a digital camera with support.

Areas of Learning: Expressive Arts and Design

Children have the opportunity to:

- Understand that different media can be combined to create new effects.
- Experiment with colour, pattern and design.
- Select appropriate materials and adapt work where necessary.
- Manipulate materials to achieve a planned effect.

A satisfying surface to work on

- Are there opportunities for children to observe and track what happens to their pictures as the water dries?

Questions for the children:

- How do your shapes stick to the glass?

- What other materials could you use?

- How does the weight of the material affect it?

- What other surfaces would you like to create art work on?

> "I have made a T for my name out of the glittery shapes."

> "It's too heavy to use on the window, it won't stick."

How does the activity enable children to develop and demonstrate the characteristics of effective learning?

Characteristic of effective learning	The enabling environment: Window art
Playing and exploring – engagement ● Finding out and exploring. ● Playing with what they know. ● Being willing to 'have a go'.	Children have the opportunity to investigate how you can combine different materials, explore the effects and ask questions about the process.
Active learning – motivation ● Being involved and concentrating. ● Keeping trying. ● Enjoying achieving what they set out to do.	Children will be motivated to create art work on an unusual surface. With no end product and an abundance of materials to work with, the opportunities for creativity are endless.
Creating and thinking critically – thinking ● Having their own ideas. ● Making links. ● Choosing ways to do things.	Whilst the water acts as glue, it is only temporary and so the children can rework and adapt their work freely. Children have the opportunity to investigate a variety of possible collage materials, testing out how they react with the water and deciding whether or not they would make effective materials for the activity.

There's no need for a clean sheet of paper each time. Just dry the glass and start again.

Homemade watercolours

Ice paint

 "This is slippery painting."

Setting up the provision

Method

Fill an ice cube tray with water and carefully drop food colouring into each cube, using a variety of colours. Place wooden lolly sticks into the water in each section and freeze. In addition, you can provide a tray of uncoloured ice cubes and water colour paints to provide children with an opportunity to paint on ice cubes as well as painting with them.

Resources

- Ice cube trays
- Water
- Food colouring
- Wooden lolly sticks
- Water colour paints
- Paint brushes
- Paper.

Handy hints

- Dip the ice cubes in water as you paint with them to help draw out more of the colour.

- Swap the wooden lolly stick handles for corks or use pre-made ice lolly moulds.

- Freeze large containers of water to create big blocks of ice for painting on.

- Create 3D ice shapes for mathematical investigations, using different shaped ice trays.

How does the activity enable children to develop and demonstrate the characteristics of effective learning?

Characteristic of effective learning	The enabling environment: Ice paint
Playing and exploring – engagement ● Finding out and exploring. ● Playing with what they know. ● Being willing to 'have a go'.	The combination of materials provided is intriguing and exciting, encouraging children to try out the activity. They will enjoy engaging in the familiar activity of painting using the unusual resources.
Active learning – motivation ● Being involved and concentrating. ● Keeping trying. ● Enjoying achieving what they set out to do.	Children have the opportunity to maintain their attention as they explore the effectiveness of their ice paint brushes. The smooth glide of the ice paint over the paper creates a unique sensation for the children to experience and talk about.
Creating and thinking critically – thinking ● Having their own ideas. ● Making links. ● Choosing ways to do things.	Children have the opportunity to explore freezing and melting. They can observe and discuss what happens to the ice paint over time and how this either inhibits or enhances its effectiveness as a painting tool.

Wet paint!

Chapter 4: Creativity

How the activity can support children's development across the 7 areas of learning

Areas of Learning: Personal, Social and Emotional Development

Children have the opportunity to:

- Share resources.
- Select and use resources with help.
- Express their own ideas and preferences.

Areas of Learning: Communication and Language

Children have the opportunity to:

- Develop their vocabulary being introduced to key words such as *freeze, melt, solid, liquid, hot, cold, temperature, change.*
- Questions why things happen and offer explanations.
- Describe the effectiveness of the cubes as a painting tool.

Areas of Learning: Physical Development

Children have the opportunity to:

- Demonstrate control handling, assembling and manipulating small tools and materials.
- Demonstrate control using painting tools.

Areas of Learning: Literacy

Children have the opportunity to:

- Write letters on the cubes.
- Give meanings to marks as they paint.

Areas of Learning: Mathematics

Children have the opportunity to:

- Investigate capacity and volume.
- Use everyday language related to time.

Areas of Learning: Understanding the World

Children have the opportunity to:

- Make careful observations, investigating changes of state and beginning to understand about solids and liquids.

Areas of Learning: Expressive Arts and Design

Children have the opportunity to:

- Understand that different media can be combined to create new effects.
- Explore colour mixing.

Questions to help you extend the activity and to ensure challenge

Questions for you:

- Do children have the opportunity to help make the ice paints before using them?

- Are there opportunities for children to discuss and further explore colour mixing?

- Are there other opportunities for children to investigate changes of state?

Questions for the children:

- How does it feel as you paint with the ice?

- How is your ice cube paint brush changing?

- Is it easier to paint with the ice or on it?

 **"It's melting all over the paper."**

Opportunities to paint with ice cubes and on them.

From sand and water to cappuccinos and lattes.

Coffee break

Setting up the provision

Method

Arrange paper coffee cups, wooden stirrers and a selection of coffee pots, jugs and small containers on a builder's tray. Provide sand to represent the coffee, shaving foam to represent frothed milk and water in teapots.

Resources

- Paper coffee cups
- Sand
- Water
- Sugar
- Shaving foam
- Wooden stirrers
- Spoons
- Small jugs and coffee pots
- Glitter in a shaker
- Recycled milk carton.

Handy hints

- Mix water with white paint to represent milk.

- Children can use glitter in shakers to add different toppings to their drinks.

- Swap your coffee shop for a tea shop by providing tea bags, both regular and herbal.

Questions to help you extend the activity and to ensure challenge

Questions for you:

- Are there opportunities for children to write their own drinks lists?

- Could you provide a till and pretend money?

How the activity can support children's development across the 7 areas of learning

Areas of Learning: Personal, Social and Emotional Development

Children have the opportunity to:

- Have their own ideas and select materials and resources independently.
- Work on their own or collaboratively with others.
- Share resources.

Areas of Learning: Communication and Language

Children have the opportunity to:

- Follow and give simple instructions.
- Explain what they are doing as they are doing it, talking through different processes.

Areas of Learning: Physical Development

Children have the opportunity to:

- Use small tools such as scoops and stirrers.

Areas of Learning: Literacy

Children have the opportunity to:

- Write lists.
- Write instructions.

Areas of Learning: Mathematics

Children have the opportunity to:

- Explore volume and capacity.
- Measure out specific quantities e.g. 4 scoops of sand.

Areas of Learning: Understanding the World

Children have the opportunity to:

- Explain and question why things happen and how things work.
- Observe how different ingredients react with each other.

Areas of Learning: Expressive Arts and Design

Children have the opportunity to:

- Understand that different media can be combined to create new effects.
- Engage in imaginative play.

Mixing up the perfect blend.

- Are there opportunities for children to experiment with and compare different ways of creating bubbles in the 'milk'? Using a whisk for example or adding washing up liquid.

Questions for the children:

- How much does a coffee cost at your shop?

- How have you made your drink?

- Could you write a list of the drinks customers can buy at your shop?

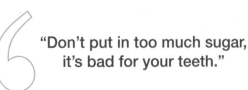

"Don't put in too much sugar, it's bad for your teeth."

"That costs 29 pence please."

How does the activity enable children to develop and demonstrate the characteristics of effective learning?

Characteristic of effective learning	The enabling environment: Coffee break
Playing and exploring – engagement ● Finding out and exploring. ● Playing with what they know. ● Being willing to 'have a go'.	The presentation of the familiar ingredients and tools is enticing, encouraging children to come and investigate. Children have the opportunity to draw on their own experiences as they play.
Active learning – motivation ● Being involved and concentrating. ● Keeping trying. ● Enjoying achieving what they set out to do.	Children have the opportunity to immerse themselves in the activity, creating their own mixtures. Children have the opportunity to try out a range of methods and techniques as they scoop, spray, plunge, pour and mix their different ingredients.
Creating and thinking critically – thinking ● Having their own ideas. ● Making links. ● Choosing ways to do things.	Children have the opportunity to follow their own paths of curiosity as they choose which ingredients and tools to use and investigate how the different ingredients combine.

Expert Baristas

Recipe challenge

Targeted areas of learning:
Mathematics and Expressive Arts
and Design

Setting up the provision

Method

Arrange a variety of cooking utensils, pots, pans and bowls on a builder's tray. Provide a variety of ingredients with opportunities to squeeze from tubes, spray from cans, scoop out of pots, shake from jars and to mix. What happens next is up to the children!

Resources

- Suggested ingredients: Dried pasta, dried lentils, dried spaghetti, dried herbs and spices, water, shaving gel, shaving foam, flour, water, toothpaste
- Spoons
- Scoops
- Spatulas
- Tongs
- Whisks
- Funnels
- Assorted plastic containers
- Baking tins
- Scales.

Handy hints

- Shaving gel works well to help bind the different ingredients together.

- Children can create their own dough with just water and flour.

- Add measuring equipment such as scales, jugs and spoons to support mathematics.

 "I have made my own mini pizza."

How does the activity enable children to develop and demonstrate the characteristics of effective learning?

Characteristic of effective learning	The enabling environment: Recipe Challenge
Playing and exploring – engagement ● Finding out and exploring. ● Playing with what they know. ● Being willing to 'have a go'.	The presentation of the familiar ingredients and tools is enticing, encouraging children to come and investigate. The activity is open-ended. There are no restrictions or limits and so children can explore, create and use their imaginations freely.
Active learning – motivation ● Being involved and concentrating. ● Keeping trying. ● Enjoying achieving what they set out to do.	Children have the opportunity to immerse themselves in the activity, creating their own mixtures and recipes. Children have the opportunity to try out a range of methods and techniques as they squeeze, spray, pour and mix their different ingredients.
Creating and thinking critically – thinking ● Having their own ideas. ● Making links. ● Choosing ways to do things.	Children have the opportunity to follow their own paths of curiosity as they choose which ingredients and tools to use and investigate how the different ingredients combine.

Enticing and open-ended

How the activity can support children's development across the 7 areas of learning

Areas of Learning: Personal, Social and Emotional Development

Children have the opportunity to:

- Have their own ideas and select materials and resources independently.
- Work on their own or collaboratively with others.
- Share resources.

Areas of Learning: Communication and Language

Children have the opportunity to:

- Follow and give simple instructions.
- Explain what they are doing as they are doing it, talking through different processes.

Areas of Learning: Physical Development

Children have the opportunity to:

- Use small tools such as scoops, stirrers and tongs.
- Mix different combinations of ingredients together.

Areas of Learning: Literacy

Children have the opportunity to:

- Write Menus.
- Write lists.
- Write instructions.

Areas of Learning: Mathematics

Children have the opportunity to:

- Explore volume and capacity.
- Measure out specific quantities e.g. 3 cups of flour.
- Use scales.

Areas of Learning: Understanding the World

Children have the opportunity to:

- Explain and question why things happen and how things work.
- Observe how different ingredients react with each other.

Areas of Learning: Expressive Arts and Design

Children have the opportunity to:

- Understand that different media can be combined to create new effects.
- Engage in imaginative play.

Questions to help you extend the activity and to ensure challenge

Questions for you:

- Are there opportunities for children to create their own menus?

- Could you develop and extend the activity creating a role play area? A cake shop, a bakery or a restaurant for example.

Questions for the children:

- What are you making?

- What happens as you mix your ingredients together?

- Which tools and ingredients have you enjoyed using the most and why?

"**I have added six scoops of flour and one big squeeze of toothpaste.**"

Master Chefs

A sensory explosion

Spice it up

Setting up the provision

Method

Choose a selection of herbs and spices and match them to earthy paint colours. Support the children to mix a teaspoon of each herb or spice with the paint, adding more to intensify the smell. Pour a heap of the herbs and spices into cake cases or small bowls so that children can add more to their paint throughout the activity. They then have the opportunity to create a picture with their new sensory paints.

Resources

- Dried herbs and spices of your choice
- Poster paint
- Paint brushes
- Tea spoon
- Paper
- Small bowls or cake cases.

Handy hints

- Try mixing fresh ingredients with the paints such as crushed garlic and grated ginger to see how these compare with the dried ingredients.

- Provide a pestle and mortar so that children can prepare their own herbs and spices.

- Grow fragrant plants in your outside area or in tubs inside to add a new sensory dimension to a variety of activities.

Questions to help you extend the activity and to ensure challenge

Questions for you:

- Have children had time to smell and discuss the herbs and spices before adding them to the paint?

How the activity can support children's development across the 7 areas of learning

Areas of Learning: Personal, Social and Emotional Development

Children have the opportunity to:
- Express their own ideas and preferences.
- Have the confidence to try new activities.

Areas of Learning: Communication and Language

Children have the opportunity to:
- Describe and compare different smells.
- Initiate and take turns in conversation.

Areas of Learning: Physical Development

Children have the opportunity to:
- Use their fingers to add pinches of herbs and spices.
- Demonstrate control when using a paintbrush.

Areas of Learning: Literacy

Children have the opportunity to:
- Give meanings to marks as they paint.

Areas of Learning: Mathematics

Children have the opportunity to:
- Measure out specific quantities e.g. 2 pinches of cinnamon.

Areas of Learning: Understanding the World

Children have the opportunity to:
- Carefully observe changes using their sense of sight and smell.

Areas of Learning: Expressive Arts and Design

Children have the opportunity to:
- Understand that different media can be combined to create new effects.
- Choose particular colours to use for a purpose.
- Explore using their sense of smell.

An extra sprinkle for good measure

- Are there opportunities for children to explore the herbs and spices further through cooking activities?

- Could children take part in a sense of smell guessing game, using a variety of food products?

- Are there opportunities for children to continue to explore mixing textures into paint? With other ingredients such as oats, flour and cereal, for example.

Questions for the children:
- Which spice do you like the smell of the most/least?

- Which smells do you recognise?

- How do the herbs and spices smell now that your painting has dried?

 "I love smelly painting."

How does the activity enable children to develop and demonstrate the characteristics of effective learning?

Characteristic of effective learning	The enabling environment: Spice it up
Playing and exploring – engagement ● Finding out and exploring. ● Playing with what they know. ● Being willing to 'have a go'.	The activity is multi-sensory and the interesting aromas will catch children's attention. Children have the opportunity to investigate with a mixture of familiar and unfamiliar materials and ingredients.
Active learning – motivation ● Being involved and concentrating. ● Keeping trying. ● Enjoying achieving what they set out to do.	The activity enables children to spend time using their sense of smell to investigate. Children have the opportunity to maintain their attention as they create paintings using their pungent sensory paints.
Creating and thinking critically – thinking ● Having their own ideas. ● Making links. ● Choosing ways to do things.	Children have the opportunity to describe how the different herbs and spices smell, making comparisons and deciding which smells they like and dislike. Children can use the different scents to inspire how and what they paint.

Potent Painting

Sensory gloves

How handy

Setting up the provision

Method

Fill several latex free gloves with your chosen materials and tie a knot in the top or secure with an elastic band. Record children's conversations to capture their use of language as they describe what they can feel.

Resources

- Latex free gloves
- Fillings for the gloves e.g. baked beans, flour, cereal, pom poms, shaving gel, shaving foam, sand, popcorn
- Funnels
- Scoops
- Elastic bands
- Camera or other recording device.

Handy hints

- Fill one of your gloves with water and freeze to create an ice hand for exploration.

- It may be easier to use a funnel when filling the gloves with some of the ingredients.

- Be careful not to over fill your gloves as some fillings will expand, such as the shaving gel.

- Use balance scales to compare the weights of the gloves.

Questions to help you extend the activity and to ensure challenge

Questions for you:

- Is key vocabulary displayed to support children's descriptions?

- Are there opportunities for children to find materials to fill their own gloves?

How does the activity enable children to develop and demonstrate the characteristics of effective learning?

Characteristic of effective learning	The enabling environment: How handy
Playing and exploring – engagement ● Finding out and exploring. ● Playing with what they know. ● Being willing to 'have a go'.	Children have the opportunity to explore different textures without getting their hands messy, which may feel safer for some children. Children have the opportunity to discover familiar materials presented in a different way.
Active learning – motivation ● Being involved and concentrating. ● Keeping trying. ● Enjoying achieving what they set out to do.	The activity enables children to spend time using their sense of touch to investigate.
Creating and thinking critically – thinking ● Having their own ideas. ● Making links. ● Choosing ways to do things.	Children have the opportunity to describe how the hands feel, making comparisons with other objects and deciding which textures they like and dislike. Children can decide and test out the best way to fill the gloves with their chosen ingredients.

Prod and poke, squish and squeeze

How the activity can support children's development across the 7 areas of learning

Areas of Learning: Personal, Social and Emotional Development
Children have the opportunity to:
- Express their own opinions.
- Initiate conversation and take into account what others say.
- Share resources.

Areas of Learning: Communication and Language
Children have the opportunity to:
- Develop their vocabulary being introduced to key words such as *texture, soft, hard, crunchy, smooth, bumpy, rough.*
- Describe how something feels.
- Listen and respond to the ideas of others.

Areas of Learning: Physical Development
Children have the opportunity to:
- Handle objects safely and with increasing control.
- Develop the strength in their hands by pinching and squeezing.

Areas of Learning: Literacy
Children have the opportunity to:
- Write down their descriptions.
- Write labels.

Areas of Learning: Mathematics
Children have the opportunity to:
- Compare and order the hands by weight.
- Use balance scales.

Areas of Learning: Understanding the World
Children have the opportunity to:
- Observe changes to materials.

Areas of Learning: Expressive Arts and Design
Children have the opportunity to:
- Be interested in and describe the texture of things.
- Manipulate materials and observe any changes they make such as impression and indentations.

- Could you use opaque gloves to challenge children to try to guess the contents just using their sense of touch?

Questions for the children:
- How does it feel?

- What do you think is in each glove?

- Which glove do you like the feel of the best and why?

"This is the most squidgy thing ever."

"Let's fill one glove with little shells. That will be all lumpy."

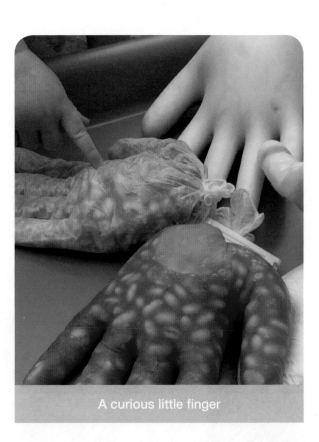

A curious little finger

Thinking outside the box

Provision inspiration

Creating enjoyable, challenging and valuable opportunities for open-ended, learning and exploration is the aim. By providing intriguing resources and materials that provoke interest and conversation we can create a rich learning environment.

There may be times when it is difficult to think of new ideas so be guided by the children. Build on their interests and plan and develop your provision accordingly.

Use familiar resources in new and unique ways and adapt and enhance activities by accessing a bank of staple resources that you build up over time. Many of these resources will be permanently accessible to children for self-selection and some can be sourced for free.

Organised and readily available resources enable you to set up and modify activities quickly and efficiently without compromising on quality. It also means that you can react to children's needs and ideas right there in the moment.

Some suggested essentials:

- Collections of natural materials such rocks, stones, fossils, shells, plants and herbs
- Assorted size containers in a variety of materials
- Clipboards and notebooks
- Colourful fabric, beads and buttons
- Paint
- Coloured sand
- Glitter
- Play animals and play people
- Clothes pegs and tweezers.

Opportunities to develop Literacy and Mathematics skills should be available across your provision, not just in designated writing or maths areas. You could provide measuring resources in your construction area for example and counting and sorting opportunities within your fine motor activities. Similarly, you could encourage story writing with books and writing tools amongst your small world and lists and diaries in your role play areas.

Conclusion

Permanent resources for writing and mark making are crucial to developing independent writers. Such resources should be available both inside and outside and across many different types of activity.
Ways to provide these opportunities include:

- Displaying whiteboards or laminated paper by water play. A splash proof and reusable resource.
- Recycling out of date diaries and calendars for use in role play areas.
- Attaching clipboards and notebooks to builder's trays and sand trays for writing inspired by sand play and small world.
- Providing a roll of thick paper outside on the ground that children can access freely.
- Providing each child with their own clipboard with their name on for writing on the move.
- Securing paper underneath climbing frames and tables for den writing.

Finally, challenge and aim high. Children amaze us with their determination, persistence, resourcefulness and creativity every day. We must reflect this in our provision and in the resources that we provide. It is crucial that children are sufficiently challenged, without this we limit how much children can learn and quickly lose their attention.

We can give children explicit challenges through questioning and setting specific goals but it is the activities that invite children to construct their own challenges that have the most impact. How we present the activities is therefore key.

A handy storage system – visible and easily accessible writing tools attached to small world.

How does the activity enable children to develop and demonstrate the characteristics of effective learning? (Fill in below)

Characteristic of effective learning	The enabling environment: _____
Playing and exploring – engagement ● Finding out and exploring. ● Playing with what they know. ● Being willing to 'have a go'.	
Active learning – motivation ● Being involved and concentrating. ● Keeping trying. ● Enjoying achieving what they set out to do.	
Creating and thinking critically – thinking ● Having their own ideas. ● Making links. ● Choosing ways to do things.	

7 areas of learning table

How the activity can support children's development across the 7 areas of learning

Areas of Learning: Personal, Social and Emotional Development

Children have the opportunity to:

-
-
-

Areas of Learning: Communication and Language

Children have the opportunity to:

-
-
-

Areas of Learning: Physical Development

Children have the opportunity to:

-
-
-

Areas of Learning: Literacy

Children have the opportunity to:

-
-
-

Areas of Learning: Mathematics

Children have the opportunity to:

-
-
-

Areas of Learning: Understanding the World

Children have the opportunity to:

-
-
-

Areas of Learning: Expressive Arts and Design

Children have the opportunity to:

-
-
-